The Tale of Two Bad Mice

The Tale of Two Bad Mice

By Beatrix Potter

THE CLASSIC

Once upon a time there was

a very beautiful doll's-house;

it was red brick with white windows,

and it had real muslin curtains and

a front door and a chimney.

It belonged to two Dolls called Lucinda

and Jane, at least it belonged to Lucinda;

but she never ordered meals.

Jane was the Cook; but she never

did any cooking, because the dinner

had been bought ready-made,

in a box full of shavings.

Provisions.
6ᵈ

There were two red lobsters

and a ham, a fish, a pudding,

and some pears and oranges.

They would not come off the plates,

but they were extremely beautiful.

One morning Lucinda and Jane had gone

out for a drive in the doll's perambulator.

There was no one in the nursery,

and it was very quiet.

Presently there was a little scuffling,

scratching noise in a corner near

the fire-place, where there was

a hole under the skirting-board.

Tom Thumb put out his head for a moment,

and then popped it in again.

Tom Thumb was a mouse.

A minute afterwards, Hunca Munca,

his wife, put her head out, too;

and when she saw that there was

no one in the nursery, she ventured

out on the oilcloth under the coal-box.

The doll's-house stood at the other
side of the fire-place.

Tom Thumb and Hunca Munca went
cautiously across the hearthrug.

They pushed the front door—
it was not fast.

Tom Thumb and Hunca Munca went

upstairs and peeped into the dining-room.

Then they squeaked with joy!

Such a lovely dinner was laid out

upon the table!

There were tin spoons,

and lead knives and forks,

and two dolly-chairs—all *so* convenient!

Tom Thumb set to work at once

to carve the ham.

It was a beautiful shiny yellow,

streaked with red.

The knife crumpled up and hurt him;

he put his finger in his mouth.

"It is not boiled enough; it is hard.

You have a try, Hunca Munca."

Hunca Munca stood up in her chair,

and chopped at the ham with

another lead knife.

"It's as hard as the hams at the

cheesemonger's," said Hunca Munca.

The ham broke off the plate with a jerk,
and rolled under the table.

"Let it alone," said Tom Thumb;

"give me some fish, Hunca Munca!"

Hunca Munca tried every tin spoon in turn;

the fish was glued to the dish.

Then Tom Thumb lost his temper.

He put the ham in the middle of the floor,

and hit it with the tongs and with the shovel—

bang, bang, smash, smash!

The ham flew all into pieces,

for underneath the shiny paint

it was made of nothing but plaster!

Then there was no end to the rage and

disappointment of Tom Thumb and Hunca Munca.

They broke up the pudding, the lobsters,

the pears and the oranges.

As the fish would not come off the plate,

they put it into the red-hot crinkly paper

fire in the kitchen; but it would not burn either.

Tom Thumb went up the kitchen

chimney and looked out at the top —

there was no soot.

While Tom Thumb was up the chimney,

Hunca Munca had another disappointment.

She found some tiny canisters upon the

dresser, labelled— Rice— Coffee —Sago—

but when she turned them upside down,

there was nothing inside except

red and blue beads.

SAGO
TAPIOCA
CURRANTS
RICE

Then those mice set to work to do all the mischief they could—especially Tom Thumb!

He took Jane's clothes out of the chest of drawers in her bedroom, and he threw them out of the top floor window.

But Hunca Munca had a frugal mind.

After pulling half the feathers out of Lucinda's bolster, she remembered that she herself was in want of a feather bed.

With Tom Thumbs's assistance

she carried the bolster downstairs,

and across the hearthrug.

It was difficult to squeeze

the bolster into the mouse-hole;

but they managed it somehow.

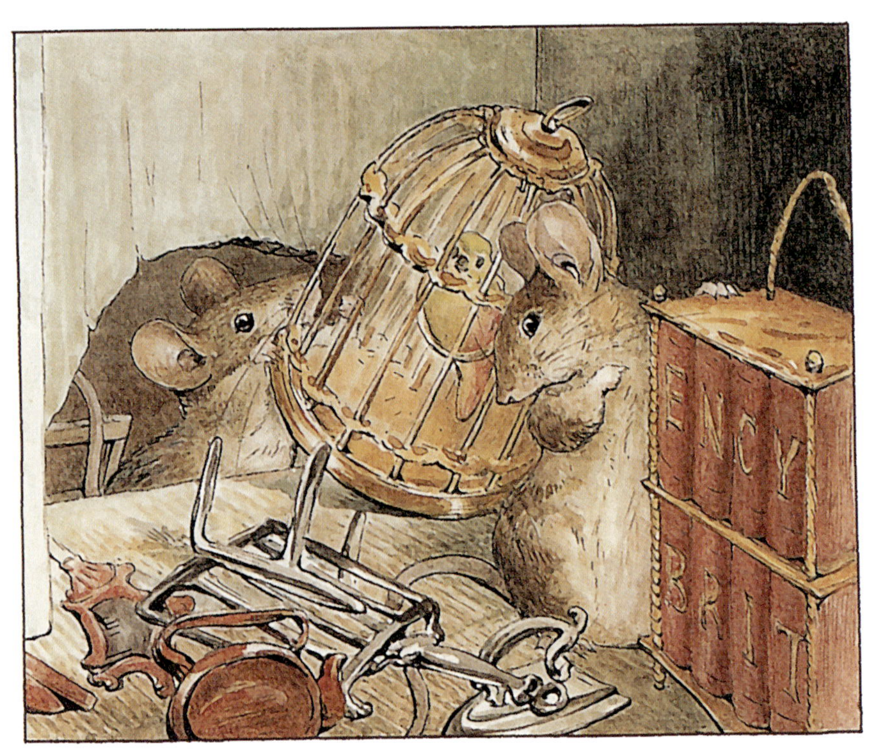

Then Hunca Munca went back
and fetched a chair, a book-case,
a bird-cage, and several small
odds and ends.

The book-case and
the bird-cage refused to go
into the mouse-hole.

Hunca Munca left them behind the coal-box,

and went to fetch a cradle.

Hunca Munca was just returning with another chair, when suddenly there was a noise of talking outside upon the landing.

The mice rushed back to their hole, and the dolls came into the nursery.

What a sight met the eyes of

Jane and Lucinda!

Lucinda sat upon the upset kitchen

stove and stared; and Jane leant against

the kitchen dresser and smiled—

but neither of them made any remark.

The book-case and the bird-cage

were rescued from under the

coal-box—but Hunca Munca has

got the cradle, and some of

Lucinda's clothes.

She also has some useful pots and pans,

and several other things.

The little girl that the doll's-house

belonged to, said—

"I will get a doll dressed like a policeman!"

But the nurse said—

"I will set a mouse-trap!"

So that is the story of the two Bad Mice,—

but they were not so very very

naughty after all, because

Tom Thumb paid for everything he broke.

He found a crooked sixpence under

the hearth-rug; and upon Christmas Eve,

he and Hunca Munca stuffed it into

one of the stockings of Lucinda and Jane.

And very early every morning—

before anybody is awake—

Hunca Munca comes with her

dust-pan and her broom to

sweep the dollies' house!

The Tale of Two Bad Mice
by Beatrix Potter

Published by The Classic Publishing Co.
ⓒ The Classic Publishing 2013

The Classic in Mirbookcompany Publishing Co. Ltd.
239-18, Yeonnam-dong, Mapo-gu, Seoul, Korea
Telephone : 02-3141-4421 Fax : 02-3141-4428
Web site : cafe.naver.com/mirbookcompany
E-mail : sanhonjinju@naver.com